Get pupils' knowledge in order with CGP!

Looking for a simple way to help pupils learn all the key facts and methods for Year 5 English? Well, look no further — this Knowledge Organiser is the perfect solution!

We've condensed each topic down to the essentials, so it covers exactly what pupils need, with clear examples and tables.

And that's not all! There's a matching Year 5 English Knowledge Retriever — a great way of making sure pupils have got to grips with the content of every page.

CGP – still the best! ☺

Our sole aim here at CGP is to produce the highest quality books — carefully written, immaculately presented and dangerously close to being funny.

Then we work our socks off to get them out to you — at the cheapest possible prices.

Published by CGP.

Editors: Siân Butler, Robbie Driscoll, Nathan Mair, Georgina Paxman, James Summersgill

With thanks to Catherine Heygate and Amanda MacNaughton for the proofreading.

With thanks to Alice Dent for the copyright research.

ISBN: 978 1 78908 961 5

Printed by Elanders Ltd, Newcastle upon Tyne.
Clipart from Corel®

Based on the classic CGP style created by Richard Parsons.

Contents

Grammar Basics

Nouns

Nouns: words that name things

Noun Type	Used to name...	Examples
Concrete	things you see, touch, smell or hear	mouse, cheese
Abstract	ideas or feelings	love, positivity
Collective	groups of people or things	a swarm of bees

Verbs

Verbs: doing or being words

> Iris plays chess.

Verbs change depending on who is doing the action.

> I walk.
> He walks.
> They walk.

Irregular verbs change in different ways. E.g. 'I am', 'she is'.

Adjectives

Adjectives tell you more about a noun.

> the creaky stairs   a quiet girl

Modal verbs: show how certain or possible something is

> I might paint.   I will paint.

Adverbs

Adverbs can describe:

1. **Verbs** — She calmly slept in bed.

2. **Adjectives** — He is very loud.

3. **Adverbs** — I spoke really quietly.

Adverbs can also show possibility.

It is clearly lazy.

Pronouns

Pronouns replace nouns.

Henrik baked a cake, and he decorated it.

Determiners

Determiners go in front of nouns.

They tell you if a noun is a general or specific thing.

I found a key.

I ate an orange.

I played my guitar.

I fixed this bike.

Clauses

Main clause: has a subject and a verb, and makes sense on its own

Subordinate clause: gives extra information but doesn't make sense on its own

EXAMPLE

Fred looked pleased when the sun started to appear.

Relative Clauses

Relative clause: a subordinate clause often introduced by a <u>relative pronoun</u>

This is the best view <u>that</u> I've seen.

Relative clauses don't always have a <u>relative pronoun</u>.

Geography is the subject <u>that</u> I enjoy the most.

You can remove the word 'that' and the sentence would still make sense.

Phrases

Phrase: a group of words with either no verb, no subject or neither

to the front

Noun phrase: contains a noun and any words that describe it

the enormous red sunflower outside

Pronouns avoid repeating 'Henrik' and 'cake'.

Relative pronouns introduce relative clauses.

I saw the girl <u>who</u> was crying.

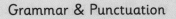

Tenses & Linking Words

Conjunctions

Co-ordinating conjunctions join two main clauses.

Use **FANBOYS** to remember them:

For And Nor But Or Yet So

> **EXAMPLE**
> I visited Iceland **but** I didn't see any ice.

main clauses

Conjunctions can help your writing to flow. This is called cohesion.

> The café closed. The chef was ill. There was no coffee left.

> The café closed **because** the chef was ill **and** there was no coffee left.

Subordinating conjunctions

Subordinating conjunctions can go at the start of a sentence or in the middle.

introduce a subordinate clause.

main clause

> **EXAMPLE**
> Lois likes to read **while** she brushes her teeth.

subordinate clause

Prepositions

Prepositions can tell you:

1 Where things are
Pip is **on** the rock.

2 When something happens
We stayed up **until** sunset.

3 Why something happens
We hid **because of** the rain.

Linking Ideas & Paragraphs

Adverbial phrases tell you how, when, where or how often something happens.

You can use adverbial phrases to make your sentences flow smoothly:

> Tomorrow evening, we're going to Inverness. We'll stop in Edinburgh on the way.

Present Tense & Past Tense

Use the simple present tense to write about something that happens regularly.

Raj dances.

Connie draws.

Raj danced.

Connie drew.

Use the simple past tense to write about something that's finished.

Verbs with 'ing'

To write about something that's still happening, use the present form of 'to be' plus the main verb with 'ing' on the end.

are / am / is verb ing I am cooking an omelette.

'ing' verbs in the past are formed in the same way, but 'to be' has to be in the past tense.

They were frowning.

You can also use adverbs and adverbial phrases to link paragraphs together smoothly.

EXAMPLE

Lola peered into the butterfly house through a tiny crack in the door.

Inside the butterfly house, butterflies of all shapes and sizes fluttered gracefully.

The Present Perfect

The present perfect describes something that happened recently.

I have lost my key.

Use the present tense of 'to have' and a past tense form of the main verb.

He has seen a robin.

The main verb is often the same as the normal past tense, but not always.

Punctuation Basics

Capital Letters

Always start a sentence with a capital letter.

Use capital letters for the word 'I' and for names of places and people.

> Next Friday, I am going to Norway.

Commas in Lists

Use commas to separate items in a list.

Ending a Sentence

- Statements often end in a full stop.

  It's sunny today.

? Questions always end in a question mark.

  How are you?

! Exclamations, some commands, and sentences that are said loudly or with strong emotion end in an exclamation mark.

  That's fantastic!

  Watch out!

Commas After...

Subordinate clauses

Only use a comma when the subordinate clause comes before the main clause.

Before I fall asleep, I count sheep.

Fronted adverbials

You need a comma when the adverbial phrase is at the start of the sentence.

In the garden, there's a hungry dog.

Add a comma between each item in a list except the last two.

Separate the last two things with 'and' or 'or'.

EXAMPLE

I ate two apples, five cherries, seven raspberries and one banana today.

Commas to Avoid Ambiguity

Use commas to make the meaning of a sentence clearer.

Otis asked his parents, Anna and Fiona.

This suggests Otis's parents are called Anna and Fiona.

Otis asked his parents, Anna, and Fiona.

This suggests Otis asked his parents, as well as Anna and Fiona.

It's OK to put a comma before 'and' if the sentence is confusing without one.

Paragraphs

Use a new paragraph for a:

1 new speaker

2 new time

3 new place

4 new subject

"Look!" squealed Olivia. "Can you see them?"

"They're so cute! I've never seen a fox in the daytime before," replied Tommasso.

The next day, they set up a camera in the garden to try to record the fox and her cubs.

At school, Olivia struggled to contain her excitement and couldn't wait to go home to check the footage. It was difficult to concentrate in lessons and she accidentally wrote the word 'fox' instead of 'box'.

Another thing distracting her was the thought of digging into her cheese sandwiches at lunchtime. She breathed a sigh of relief when the lunch bell rang.

More Punctuation

Adding Extra Information

Add extra information to a sentence using pairs of:

1 Commas I had a hot chocolate, my favourite drink, to warm up.

2 Brackets Bess (our first pet) was a black labrador.

The extra information is sometimes called a parenthesis.

3 Dashes At the park — the one by the river — we had a picnic.

The punctuation goes on either side of the extra information.

The sentence should still make sense when the extra information is removed.

Apostrophes

Missing letters

The apostrophe shows where you've left letters out of a shortened word.

he is → he's   they are → they're

Use of apostrophes

Plural possession

Use apostrophes to show possession for plural nouns.

If the plural noun ends in 's', you only add an apostrophe.

the piglets' mother

Single possession

To show that someone or something owns something, add an apostrophe and 's'.

For singular nouns, you always add the 's', even if the word ends in 's' already.

the dog's nose   the bus's wheels

Its & It's

'its' and 'it's' mean two different things:

its = 'belonging to it'   The duck washed its feet.

it's = 'it is' or 'it has'   It's a scary film.   It's been tiring.

Inverted Commas & Punctuating Speech

If speech starts part-way through the sentence, add a comma before it.

Speech always ends with a punctuation mark, which goes inside the inverted commas.

If the plural noun doesn't end in 's', add an apostrophe and 's'.

the people's beliefs

Keith asked, "What's for tea?"

Inverted commas are also known as speech marks.

Speech usually starts with a capital letter, even when it isn't at the start of a sentence.

Punctuating Speech in Two Parts

Sometimes, speech is broken up by other information.

Don't forget to add punctuation at the end of your sentence.

"I want one thing," said Lyla, "and that's ice cream!"

The sentence hasn't finished yet, so you need a comma.

You need a comma before the second bit of speech.

You don't need a capital letter if the second bit of speech is part of the same sentence.

Prefixes, Suffixes & Word Endings

Key Words

Prefix: a letter or group of letters added to the start of a word

Suffix: a letter or group of letters added to the end of a word

Root word: the word a prefix or suffix is added to

'shul', 'shun' & 'shus'

1 The '**shul**' sound is often spelt:

'tial' after a consonant ➡️ **par**tial

'cial' after a vowel ➡️ **spe**cial

Hyphenating Prefixes

Use a hyphen to add a prefix:

1 to avoid confusion with similar words.

> **EXAMPLE**
>
> 're-sent' means 'sent again'.
>
> I re-sent the email.
>
> I resent eating greens.

'resent' means 'to feel bitter towards something'.

Prefixes

> The spelling of the root word does not change when a prefix is added.

Prefix	Meaning	Example
under	too little	underfund
over	too much	overslept
non	not	nonsense
mid	middle	midway
pre, fore	before	preschool, forecast
en, em	to put into	encircle, embrace

> 'em' is used instead of 'en' when the root word starts with 'b' or 'p'.

co-exist

2 if the prefix ends in a vowel and the root word begins with a vowel.

2 The '**shun**' sound is spelt:

There are some exceptions to these rules.

Root word ends...	Ending	Examples
't' or 'te'	'tion'	completion, action
'c' or 'cs'	'cian'	clinician, politician
'd', 'de' or 'se'	'sion'	television, decision
'ss' or 'mit'	'ssion'	submission, discussion

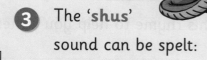

3 The '**shus**' sound can be spelt:

cious ➡ vicious

tious ➡ nutritious

If the root word ends in 'ce', the 'shus' sound is usually spelt 'cious'.

space ➡ spacious

More Word Endings

Sometimes, word endings sound similar, but are spelt differently.

The '**unce**' sound

balance   science

The '**unt**' sound

distant   talent

The '**uncy**' sound

vacancy   currency

'**able**', '**ible**', '**ably**' and '**ibly**'

reliable   horrible

reliably   horribly

Suffixes

Sometimes, the root word doesn't change when you add a suffix...

EXAMPLE

social + ise ➡ socialise

Nouns and adjectives often turn into verbs when suffixes are added to them.

...but other times, it does change.

EXAMPLE

terror + ify ➡ terrify

EXAMPLE

active + ate ➡ activate

Confusing Words

'ei' & 'ie' Words

Use this rhyme to help you remember how to spell 'ei' and 'ie' words:

> 'i' before 'e' except after 'c' if the vowel sound rhymes with bee.

shriek — Rhymes with bee and doesn't follow a 'c', so 'i' before 'e'.

receive — Rhymes with bee but follows a 'c', so 'e' before 'i'.

society — Doesn't rhyme with bee but follows a 'c', so 'i' before 'e'.

Some words don't follow the rule, e.g. seize. You just have to learn these words.

'ough' Words

Words containing the letters 'ough' can sound very different. For example:

Here the 'ough' sounds like 'oh'. **dough, although**

Here the 'ough' sounds like 'or'. **thought, nought**

Here the 'ough' sounds like 'uff'. **rough, enough**

Here the 'ough' sounds like 'ow'. **drought, plough**

Homophones

Homophones: words that sound the same, but have different meanings and spellings

Silent Letters

Silent letters: letters that you don't hear when you say a word

lamb	silent 'b'
listen	silent 't'
gnome	silent 'g'
write	silent 'w'
knee	silent 'k'
wheat	silent 'h'
island	silent 's'
column	silent 'n'

These are just examples — other letters can be silent too.

Unstressed Vowels

Unstressed vowels: vowel sounds that you can't hear clearly

Sometimes they sound like a different vowel:

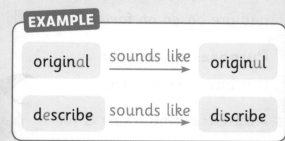

EXAMPLE

original → sounds like → originul

describe → sounds like → discribe

Sometimes they sound like they're not there at all:

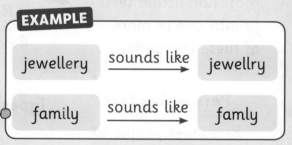

EXAMPLE

jewellery → sounds like → jewellry

family → sounds like → famly

---

past: the time gone by

passed: went by

---

past vs. passed

People did different jobs in the past.

I passed my friend's house earlier.

Types of Text

See p.18-19 for more on features of stories.

Key Words

Fiction: texts about imaginary people and events

Non-fiction: texts that contain information and are based on facts

Purpose: the reason a text has been written

Audience: who a text is for

Stories

Key features of stories:

- Usually have a main character and often a villain.
- Have a beginning, a middle and an end.
- The purpose of stories is often to entertain the reader.

There are many types of stories.

Types of Non-Fiction

Most non-fiction texts fit into one or more of these categories.

Recount
Retells events

Discussion text
Shares arguments for and against a topic

Persuasive text
Persuades people to think or do something

Types of non-fiction

Instruction text
Tells people how to do something

Explanation text
Explains how a process works

Report
Gives information on a topic, often in non-chronological order

Non-chronological means 'not in time order'.

EXAMPLE

1. An article debating whether phones should be allowed in school
2. A fact file about Tudor Britain

Myths

- explain ideas from the natural world
- characters are often gods or magical beings

Adventure stories

- main character goes on a mission
- often involve danger and excitement

Science fiction

- often set in the future or a different world
- plots use ideas from science and technology

→ Discussion text

→ Report

Other Types of Fiction

Poems	often arranged into verses
	use techniques like rhyme and repetition
Plays	designed to be performed
	include dialogue (characters talking)
	stage directions to tell the actors what to do

Identifying Themes

Themes: the key ideas or messages in a text

Look for:

1 ideas that appear multiple times.

2 important topics.

EXAMPLE

Text: The Owl and the Pussy-Cat (nonsense poem)

Plot: An owl and a pussy-cat fall in love and get engaged on a boat. They buy a ring from a pig and get married.

Themes: love, marriage

Reading Skills

Working Out Meanings

If you're not sure what a word or phrase means:

1. Find clues in the text — other words you do understand.
2. See if it's part of a word family — use this to guess the meaning.
3. Look it up in a dictionary.

Language & Structure

Language

What effect do words and phrases have?

> Wrinkling her brow, Ria spoke through gritted teeth.

These words and phrases make Ria sound annoyed.

Finding Information

Information can be stated directly:

> Mount Everest is the highest point on Earth, reaching a height of 8849 metres.

The text tells you that Mount Everest is 8849 metres high.

Or you might have to use clues to work it out:

> Zayn smiled when he saw a red squirrel sprint across the garden.

The text tells you that Zayn "smiled". This clue suggests he feels happy.

Summarising Texts

Summarise the main message or ideas of a text.

> Paragraph 1: Rome has lots to do.
> Paragraph 2: It has delicious food.
> Paragraph 3: The people are nice.

Summary: Rome is a great place to visit.

Structure

1. How are the ideas grouped together?

2. Are there any points where things change?

3. What order are events described in?

Facts & Opinions

Facts: statements backed up by statistics or evidence

> Polar bears can swim at speeds of up to 6 mph in water.

This information can be proven with evidence.

Opinions: personal views

> I think oranges are delicious.

opinion word

> Everyone loves oranges.

Opinions often use exaggerated language.

Comparing Texts

Make comparisons by looking for similarities and differences within or between texts.

Things you could compare:

1. the key themes
2. the use of language
3. characters — how they act and feel

Making Predictions

When making predictions, think about:

What has happened so far?

How are the characters feeling?

Are there clues about what's next?

> Wei pitched the tent and then glanced up to the sky. A large, grey cloud loomed above him.

The "large, grey cloud" that "loomed above" suggests it is about to rain.

Writing Fiction

Planning

Always plan before you start writing. Think about:

1 | What? | plot   **2** | Where? | setting   **3** | Who? | characters

Plot

Basic story structure:

Beginning	the scene is set
Middle	a problem or conflict
End	the problem is fixed

Setting

Use descriptive language to set the scene:

adjective   verb

EXAMPLE

The stormy **waves** crashed onto the shore powerfully.

adverb

Starting a Story

Two great ways to begin:

1 in the middle of the action

> Alvanah sprinted frantically away from the ghostly bat, trying not to anger it further.

2 with a character speaking

> "What was that noise?" Kareem asked timidly.

You can use speech to show a character's personality.

Simile: when you say something is like something else

> Leo ran as fast as a cheetah.

Checking Your Writing

Always check for errors, and correct mistakes neatly.

> was
> It ~~were~~ raining cats and dogs.

Characters

Show their personality...

> **EXAMPLE**
>
> Ruby shuffled nervously into the room, anxiously playing with her long, curly hair.

...and their appearance.

Language Techniques

Onomatopoeia: when a word sounds like what it describes

> Rex growled at the postman.

Metaphor: when you say something is something else

> Abeke's story was a tangled web.

Common mistakes:

1. verb not matching the subject
2. not staying in the same tense
3. forgetting to use paragraphs

Synonyms

Use a thesaurus to find interesting synonyms of common words.

> Synonyms are words with similar meanings.

> Synonyms of 'scary'
>
> terrifying
>
> frightening
>
> horrifying

Story Writing Checklist

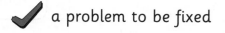

Make sure your story has:

- ✔ interesting characters & setting
- ✔ a problem to be fixed
- ✔ an effective start & ending
- ✔ descriptive language
- ✔ correct spelling & grammar

Writing Non-Fiction

Formal Writing

1 uses formal language

e.g. They were magnificent.

2 avoids contracted forms

e.g. We will speak tomorrow.

3 avoids exclamation marks

e.g. I started a new school.

Informal Writing

1 uses chatty language

e.g. They were great.

2 can use contracted forms

e.g. We'll speak tomorrow.

3 can use exclamation marks

e.g. I started a new school!

In informal writing you can add questions to the end of sentences, e.g. 'You like rock music, don't you?'

Informal Letters

Informal letters use a chatty and friendly style.

Use a new paragraph for each new point in a letter.

Their first name

13 Dreary Lane
13th December

Your address

Hello Joe,
    I wanted to tell you my news!

Lots of love,
Calum

Your first name   Friendly ending

Formal Letters

Formal letters follow strict rules.

Their name and address

Your address

2 Robin Street
28th June

Penny Black
8 Peacock Crescent

Dear Mrs Black,
    I am writing to congratulate you on...

Yours sincerely,
Mr Bright   Your title and surname

Begin with your reason for writing.

Standard English

Always use Standard English in your writing.

Non-Standard English	Standard English
I seen my favourite film.	I saw my favourite film.
I ain't tried snorkelling.	I haven't tried snorkelling.
Ben didn't want nothing.	Ben didn't want anything.

Writing Information Texts

Layout devices make your writing clearer and more appealing.

Slogan

Subheading

If you don't know their name, begin your letter with 'Dear Sir/Madam' and end it with 'Yours faithfully'.

Heading

Bake with Badra

Bake it better

Underlining

<u>Brush up on your baking skills</u>
From whipping up a Victoria sponge to crafting perfect chocolate chip cookies, Badra will teach you to become a master baker in no time.

- 1 hour lesson — £20
- 2 hour lesson — £30

Bullet points

Index